Claire Bear Flies to Oshkosh

Written by Sue Hughes
Illustrated by Linda Terentiak

Published by
Powder Puff Pilot

Claire Bear Flies to Oshkosh
Written by Sue Hughes
Illustrated by Linda Terentiak
Copyright 2013 by Sue Hughes

Published by:
Powder Puff Pilot
2367 Waynoka Street
Waynoka, OK 73860

www.PowderPuffPilot.com

Printed in the United States of America

Third Printing

ISBN: 978-0-9845579-5-0

For seven days every summer, the Experimental Aircraft Association (EAA) transforms Wittman Airport in Oshkosh, Wisconsin from an average municipal airport to the busiest airport on the planet! That's when EAA hosts AirVenture, the world's biggest celebration of all things aviation.

Air traffic controllers have devised unique arrival and departure procedures to handle the heavy traffic converging on Oshkosh that week. Claire uses these special procedures to fly into Oshkosh for her big AirVenture debut!

Throughout the story, look for the pilot glossary words in red. They are defined at the end of the story on pages 40 to 42.

When Claire Bear went to her mailbox one day
She spotted a letter from the EAA.

4

It said, "Come fly in our air show this year."
Claire jumped up and down and let out a big cheer.

EAA

Dear Claire Bear,

Come fly in our air show this year!

EAA AirVenture
Oshkosh, Wisconsin

5

Anyone who flies or is in aviation
Knows that Oshkosh hosts the world's biggest celebration.

Claire Bear is an airshow performer, you know,
But only the best are invited to the Oshkosh airshow.

7

"EAA AirVenture, I'm on my way!"
Claire said, and started planning that very same day.

8

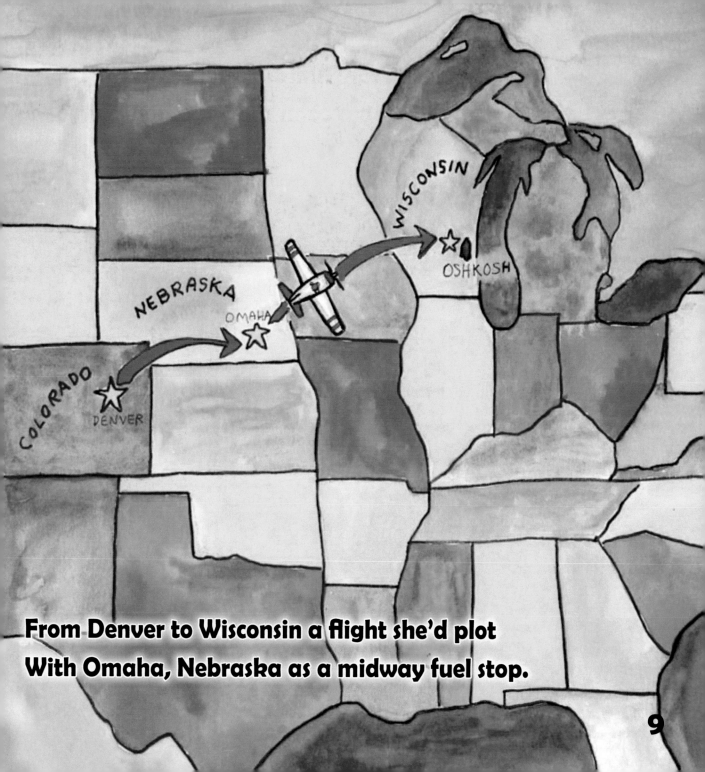

From Denver to Wisconsin a flight she'd plot
With Omaha, Nebraska as a midway fuel stop.

She departed for Oshkosh as early as she could.
The wind was calm and weather was good.

Over farms and cities, Claire stayed on track.
She crossed the Mississippi with a tailwind at her back.

11

For one week every year, come rain or come sun,
Oshkosh has the world's busiest airport, bar none.

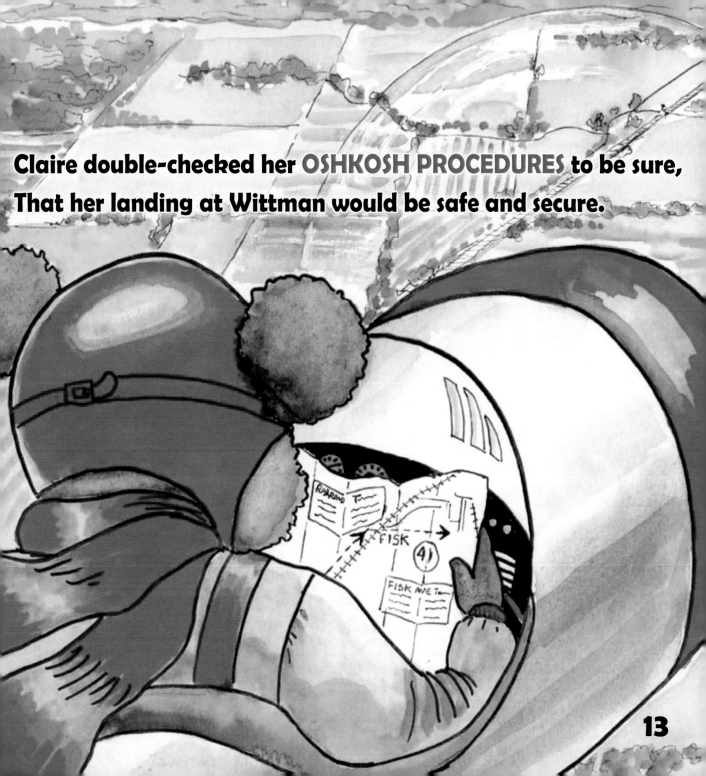

Claire double-checked her OSHKOSH PROCEDURES to be sure,
That her landing at Wittman would be safe and secure.

Getting closer to Oshkosh, her excitement grew,
She tuned into APPROACH so she'd know what to do.

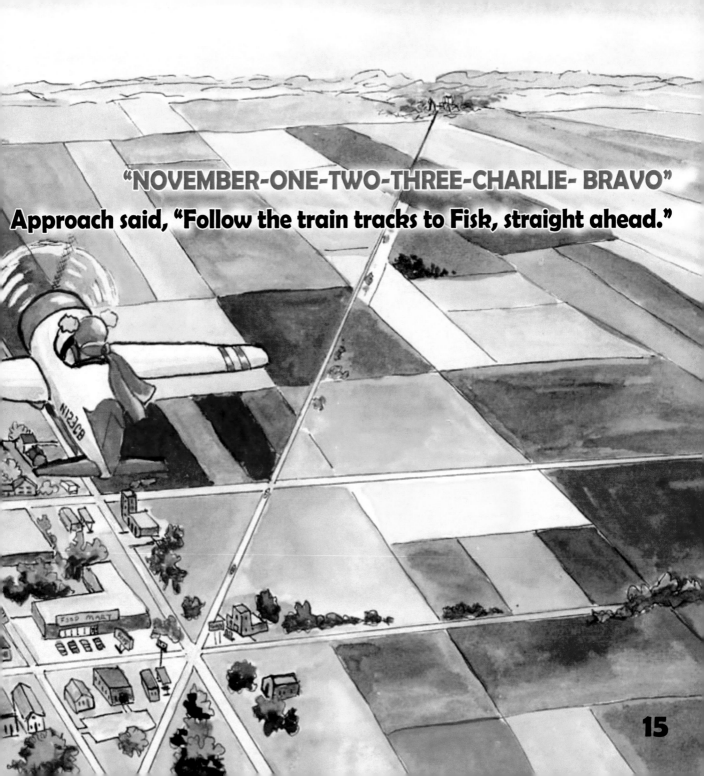

At Fisk, Approach said, "Tune into the TOWER, Expect TWO SEVEN." She pulled back on the power.

At a thousand feet high, with the airport in sight,
Claire turned DOWNWIND with her runway to the right.

"ROCK YOUR WINGS," Tower said, with Claire in sight.
She rolled her plane to the left and then to the right.

18

The Tower watched and then said, "Thanks a lot. Cleared to land on Two-Seven, right on the GREEN DOT."

Claire touched down with ease and the Tower said, "Turn right and then TAXI to park, straight ahead."

"I'm finally at Oshkosh!" Claire shouted, "Yippee! I can't wait to see all there is to see."

21

On the grounds were aircraft of every shape and size,
Old ones and new ones, she couldn't believe her eyes!

22

There were airplanes for sale and airplanes for show,
Airplanes in the air, and parked all in a row.

She visited the WARBIRDS from World War II
And other military planes that flew for freedom, too.

24

In the **VINTAGE** sections, the airplanes hardly looked worn,
But those antiques flew before Claire was born!

25

Visitors flew in from near and far,
From Wichita, Kansas to South Zanzibar.

26

Some camped in tents and hoped it wouldn't rain.
Some slept in a tent right next to their plane.

Helicopters circled, thrilling visitors with rides
And jumpers with parachutes floated down from the skies.

Noisy and crowded, Claire loved every minute,
But it was time for the airshow, and Claire Bear was in it!

29

She prelighted her plane, checked every last part,
And asked the **AIR BOSS** if it was her turn to start.

"You're on, Claire Bear!" and she revved up her engine.
She let out a big breath to relieve a little tension.

She never flew for so large of a crowd.
"I can do this," she said to herself out loud.

Claire took Runway Three-Six and her confidence grew.
She rotated at 55 and off she flew.

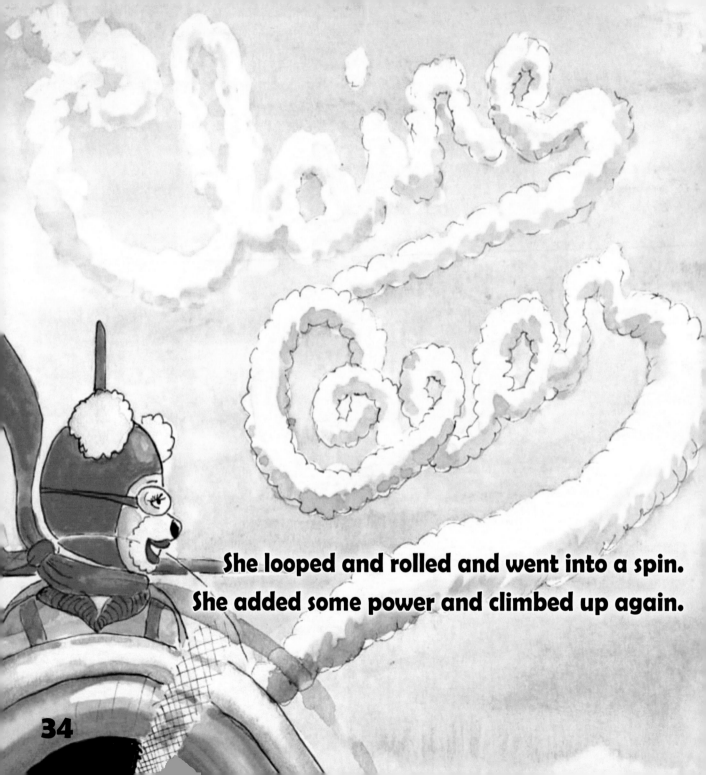

She looped and rolled and went into a spin.
She added some power and climbed up again.

34

With smoke trailing behind, she spelled out her name.
The crowd loved her act. She was so glad she came!

She finished her show and came back to the ground,
On Runway Three-Six, she gently touched down.

36

The announcer proclaimed, "That bear sure can fly!"
Claire waved to the crowd, as she was driven on by.

Claire Bear thought, as she heard her fans cheer,
"I can't wait to come to Oshkosh next year!"

38

Claire flew back to Denver, as proud as could be.
"I flew to Oshkosh! What's next for me?"

OSHKOSH GLOSSARY

AIR BOSS   Person in charge of all the aircraft operations at the show.

APPROACH   Air traffic controllers who manage aircraft by talking on the radio to pilots arriving at or departing from an airport. Pilots are directed by Approach until they get close enough to see the airport, and then they switch to the Tower.

DOWNWIND   Position in the landing traffic pattern where the aircraft is parallel to the runway in the opposite direction of landing.

GREEN DOT   Marking on the runway that enables controllers to land more than one airplane on a runway at a time, which is usually against the rules. The FAA gives controllers at AirVenture special permission, since it's so busy.

NOVEMBER-ONE-TWO-THREE-CHARLIE-BRAVO

Pilots use the pilot alphabet when communicating over the radio. In this case, Claire is telling the controller her airplane's tail number, N123CB, so the controller knows which airplane is hers.

FISK VFR Arrival to OSH

OSHKOSH PROCEDURES Since air traffic at Wittman Airport and the area surrounding Oshkosh is so busy, the FAA issues special procedures for arriving and departing during the week of AirVenture.

ROCK YOUR WINGS Direction from an air traffic controller to the pilot. Since the radios at Oshkosh are so busy, pilots rock their wings to acknowledge directions instead of answering on the radio, like they usually do.

TAXI Term for how an aircraft moves on the ground.

TOWER Air traffic controllers who manage aircraft that are landing or taking off at an airport. During AirVenture, Oshkosh has the busiest Tower in the world!

TWO-SEVEN Two-digit runway designation, named for its compass direction. In this case, the runway is aligned with 270 degrees, which means aircraft using it to land or takeoff face west.

VINTAGE Aircraft from long ago.

WARBIRDS Military aircraft from long ago.

About the Author

Claire Bear Flies to Oshkosh is the fourth children's book written by Sue Hughes, a pilot since 1996, flight instructor, and aviation technical writer. Sue taught her husband Dale to fly several years ago, and they have since purchased a Piper Arrow that they fly for business and pleasure out of Waynoka, Oklahoma.

In 2008, Sue founded Powder Puff Pilot, a company that designs and sells pilot gear and accessories for women pilots -- past, present, and future. In addition to the Claire Bear series of aviation picture books, she authors ***This Day in Women's Aviation***, a page-a-day calendar.

About the Illustrator

Linda Teretiak, a native of Waterford, Michigan, earned a Bachelor's degree in Fine Arts/Commercial Art from Central Michigan University.

In 1985, Linda attended her first air show and fell in love with aviation. She began producing aviation artwork from photographs she took whenever she went to an air show. Her hobby grew into a profession as a graphic artist when she was commissioned to create pen-and-ink drawings and watercolors for pilots and aviation enthusiasts.

Linda's first visit to EAA AirVenture in Oshkosh was in 2010, when she signed copies of the first children's book she illustrated, ***Billy's First Flight Lesson***, written by Elaine Barber. ***Claire Bear Flies to Oshkosh*** is her second children's book.

Claire Bear Flies to Oshkosh

Written by Sue Hughes
Illustrated by Linda Terentiak

Published by Powder Puff Pilot
2367 Waynoka Street
Waynoka, OK 73860

ISBN: 978-0-9845579-5-0

Order online at
www.PowderPuffPilot.com

POWDER PUFF
PILOT